Linda Mason's

Excited Ernesto

Book #5

A Spirit of Truth Storybook

Copyright Page

Excited Ernesto
Book #5
A Spirit of Truth Storybook
Author: Linda C. Mason
Published by:
Books By L Mason
P. O. Box 1162
Powhatan, VA 23139
LMasonOnTop@.com
www.BooksByLMason.com
ISBN-13: 978-1-62217-329-7
ISBN-10: 1-62217-329-5

© 2014 by Linda C. Mason
Registration # TXu 1-925-200
Illustrated by Jessica Mulles
Edited by Pastor Nona J Mason

Printed in the United States of America

Excited Ernesto

It was a boring night as I sat at home watching my uncles play dominoes. They had been at it for hours,, and I was ready to get out of there for some real excitement. The doorbell rang. It was Donté!

"Ernesto!" he said in an excited tone.

"Let's take off."

"The State Fair is in town, and I'm tired of sitting around here all day. Got some money?" he asked.

"Nope," Donté replied.

"But I can fix that," I said as I went into my bedroom and came out with $135.

I had been saving up for a particular pair of shoes, but right now, I needed to get out of this house. I was 15 years old, and Donté was 16, but neither of us had a car. The State Fair was about ten miles away, so we decided to catch the bus. Mom and Dad had given me clear instructions to be back home by 11 p.m., so if we left right away, we could still have a lot of time to have some great fun.

I was so excited thinking about finally getting away from this dull house. I could feel my energy begin to build. Donté and I had only been buddies for a short time; however, I felt very comfortable around him. Besides, he had a sister that was kind of cute --- Maria.

"What's Maria doing this evening?" I asked Donté since I had started thinking about her.

"Don't know," Donté replied.

"Who cares?" He continued. Then he turned and looked at me with that sly eye kind of look.

"Oh, yeah. You are kind of hot on Maria, aren't you, Ernesto?" He said.

"Yeah, man," I replied.

"I can't deny it. She's hot, man!" I continued.

"Ernesto! Stop talking about my sister like that! Eeeuw!" Donté said with a twisted expression on his face.

"I can't help it, man. It's so true," I interrupted.

"Okay, Ernesto. Let's change the subject!" Donté interjected.

We had only been standing at the bus stop for five minutes before the bus came. Boy, I was excited and could not wait to get to the State Fair. I had money in my pocket, and thinking about all that food made my stomach start growling.

Smothered sausages with sautéed green peppers and onions, hot dogs that never tasted like the ones you cook at home, steak and cheese sandwiches, and even bologna burgers cooked at the State Fair tasted like a million dollars! All of that cotton candy and candy apples, corn dogs on a stick, and those funnel cakes with creamy toppings were yum—my! I couldn't wait.

"Hey, man," Donté said as he nudged me back to reality.

"Are you getting on the Hurricane this time, man? If you get on it, I will, too," giving both of us a dare at the same time.

I hoped I was ready to go all the way this time. For years I'd been too chicken to get on that twisted roller coaster called the Hurricane, but now I think I might be ready to face my worst nightmare.

"Yep, I'm ready," I replied, as my thoughts moved from the yummy foods I'd been drooling over to the terror I had just committed to putting myself through. Nevertheless, there was also so much excitement in the air that I knew I would face this Hurricane with both eyes open.

As the bus neared our destination, I could see all of the high rides through the bus windows. That Ferris wheel with those high twirling swings --- and then I saw it. The Hurricane --- swooping down like a dragon as shrieks and screams filled the air. We could hear the people screaming all the way over here inside the bus. A realization hit me --- my voice will be one of those screaming very soon.

The bus came to a stop right at the gate entrance. I was so excited, and my hands were sweating. The sun had already gone down too. There was a breeze in the air with all kinds of aromas pleading for me to pig out first.

At the ticket booth, we had to purchase tickets for rides and games, and then a different kind of ticket for foods. Donté only had enough money on him for bus fare, so it was my treat today for everything else.

I purchased $50 worth of each, totaling $100, and we both headed off toward the food area. Even though we were in the food area now, we could still see and hear the action going on with the Hurricane rollercoaster. That alone kept our hearts racing, currently yearning to experience the climb to the top, and then to attempt to hold our stomachs together while swooping to the bottom at top-notch speed.

We stood in a long line to order the hot Italian sausages loaded with green peppers and onions, French fries, and a drink. My $50 in food tickets were just about gone already from that single purchase. Nevertheless, we sat down to eat while glancing around at the pretty girls. We could hear all of the other action going on around there. Traditional carnival music and excitement filled every inch of the festive park. Before I took a bite, I wondered if I should be eating this stuff just before I get on that ride. What if I spit it up? That was probably a thought that crossed my mind to tempt me to back out of my commitment. Nope! I wasn't backing out. I was sure I was going to go through with this thing tonight. I swallowed every delicious bite, and so did Donté.

"Let's go, man," I said, no longer able to contain my excitement of anticipation.

Donté wanted to play some games first. We played several games for a couple of hours, but I was too jumpy to wait any longer.

"Okay, Ernesto! Okay. We are going now! Calm down, man!" He said.

So we headed towards that extremely long line at the Hurricane gate. The line wrapped around another ride, but we got in the line anyway. We listened to all the chatter from the people in line in front of us and wished we could move up faster. Suddenly, I noticed two girls I thought I knew from our neighborhood standing about six people in front of us. Then I realized one of them was Maria, and my heart skipped a beat. I know I turned three shades of red.

"What's wrong, man?" Donté asked, noticing my new complexion shade.

"Look, Donté. There are Gloria and Maria!" I said, almost too excited to contain myself. "You wanna hook up with them to get on this ride?"

"Sure, man. Hey, Gloria! Hi Maria. I didn't know you were coming here tonight!" he yelled out.

"Are you two with anyone?"

"Hi guys," Gloria and Maria replied. "Can we come back there with you?"

"Come on!" I yelled out. As they moved back where we were in line, things became even more exciting.

"Well," Maria began, "Gloria and I were bored at the house, so we decided to have some fun at the State Fair. It looks like you guys decided to do the same thing." Maria then looked over at me and smiled.

"Have you two ladies been on the Hurricane before?" I asked, but looking directly at Maria as I did. Gloria answered instead and said no.

I grabbed Maria's hand and said, "We could pair off and protect you both on the ride, you know. Wanna get something to eat first?" I asked. Actually, I thought eating might give me more time to ease the butterflies I felt mounting in my stomach. But then a second thought, overeating, might cause me to spit up on the girls. Maria began talking first.

"No, thank you. How long have you guys been here?" she said.

"We've been here long enough to stuff down some Italian sausages loaded with green peppers and onions. But now I'm ready to do this thing!" Donté said.

"You scared?" I asked.

"Terrified!" Maria replied.

"Well, you sit with me, Maria. I'll protect you from the Big Bad Hurricane," I said.

"Yeah, right," Donté said, looking at me as he laughed. I laughed, too, because everyone knew I'd never been on this ride before; after all, I was too scared.

"Hey everybody, we are gonna do this thing together," Gloria interjected. Everyone knew that we were all scared.

After chatting for a minute or two, we noticed that the line had been moving very fast. It was almost our turn, and I felt as though I had to go to the bathroom. Wow! How disgusting! Not now, not in front of these girls, I thought.

But you know what? It would be a lot worse if I had an accident on the ride with them. I looked around and spotted a restroom right near the ride, which I thought was an excellent idea for whoever designed it that way. I excused myself from the girls for a minute and told them I'd be right back. They laughed and said, okay.

Donté and I ran over to the restroom, giggling, and in no time, we had returned with confidence, just in time to board The Hurricane.

Our position in line led us right onto the very front row of the ride.

"Oh, my goodness! Oh, my goodness!" was all I could say as we got on this thing. Maria and I took the very front seat, and Gloria and Donté were right behind us. This was going to be a ride none of us would ever forget. "Is everyone ready for this?" Gloria asked.

"Too late to back out now," I said with my stomach tied in knots about now. We felt a jerk as the Hurricane started to coast down the rail. You could hear and feel the excitement from everyone on this ride at that point because everyone started cheering with their arms whirling back and forth in the air. I looked at Maria, and she looked at me. Both of us grabbed the safety bar in front of us. We couldn't imagine how we were going to react to this adventure.

As the rollercoaster picked up speed, it banked around the first curve, and then it quickly jerked in the opposite direction. We began to climb, higher, higher, higher, as the car we were in seemed to reduce in speed. Suddenly, seemingly without warning, it banked again to the right and jerked again to the left. I looked out over the side of the car and noticed the people on the ground appeared smaller and smaller. Maria had already buried her face on my shoulder. I probably should have put my arms around her as a brave man would, but my fingers were frozen around the safety bar. I couldn't move and hoped that I wouldn't scream louder than the rest of these people. The cheers from the crowd began turning to screams. I was trying to hold it together until the car seemed to drop from under me. My screams joined the many others, as well as Maria's screams. We weren't halfway to the top yet, and I couldn't believe I was behaving like this!

And then a sense of confidence overtook me. We started climbing again, higher, even higher than before, and somewhere deep inside of me, a boldness emerged. My fingers were no longer glued to the safety bar. I nudged Maria and yelled in a loud voice so that she could hear me over all the other screams.

"Maria! Maria! Let's do this thing! Hold your head up! Come on; I'll help you hold your arms up. Take my hand!" She looked at me with a puzzled look on her face, but then with renewed confidence, she gave me her hand. As we neared the top of the highest peak of this mad ride and went over the top, we both let out a screech of real excitement - not fear. We felt as though we were falling through the air, floating down, and down --- as though we had wings.

I glanced back at Donté and Gloria. They were doing the same thing. Wow! I thought. What a rush!

"Now, let's take it in for a landing!" I yelled out loud.

As we began descending, swooping around curves and dropping to lower levels, I knew I couldn't wait to get on this thing again. We coasted to a stop, and the safety bar was released automatically. My legs were a little wobbly when I stood up, but other than that, I was pumped. I helped Maria out of the seat, and none of us could stop talking – all at the same time. We all felt the same way, and it was incredible!

We rode that Hurricane at least two more times that night and didn't even play any more games. The time was getting away from us, and we knew we had to catch the bus back home before our curfew hour, so we all sat down to eat a funnel cake as we talked about doing this all over again next year.

At home that night in bed, it was tough to sleep. The excitement of the evening had just taken over, and I had to find a way to calm myself down. I got out of bed and stood for a moment, just staring out of the window at the crystal looking full moon. The amazing glow seemed to light up the entire neighborhood. I opened my window to take in the summer breeze of this awesome night. My heart finally stopped racing, and I thought about what a wonderful life I had.

When I returned to bed this time, I only felt exhausted. I hadn't had time to think about how tired I was, but now it came and seemed to flood every muscle in my body. As I dozed off to sleep, visions of Maria seemed to rush my dreams. I was confident I would be calling on her again. For tonight, the excitement was over, but there's always tomorrow.

The End

A unique inspirational message has been coded throughout each story to help create *added focus* and a visual tool for interactive participation and concentration.

Decode your secret message and send it to me, along with your name and age, through my personal email address at LMasonOnTop@aol.com, and you will receive a personal email response from me. Additionally, a bonus finger puppet activity, along with other goodies, awaits each reader in the back of every storybook. An Editor's Edition of this 26 Storybook Collection is forthcoming, including the 26 stories within two volumes; at which time, the Master's List of every inspirational message will be revealed.

Message of Encouragement Worksheet

(You may copy this page)

(Fill in the missing letters on a <u>separate sheet of paper</u> or here, if you own the storybook, to unlock your secret message)

Excited Ernesto

_ t _ _ _ n _   _ x _ _ _ _ _   _ _ _   _ e

_ _ _ t _ g _ _ _ s   _ _ _   _ i _ _

p e _ _ _ _ ’ _   _ p _ _ _ _ _ .   W _ _ _

_ _ _   c _ _ _ _ _   s t _ _ _ _ _ _ .   _ _

_ _ _ r y _ h _ _ _   _ _ _ h   _ _ _ _

_ _ c _ _ _ _ _ n t.

Check out my website at <u>www.BooksByLMason.com</u> to find out other games, puzzles, finger puppets, and treasure hunts located within each paperback storybook, in addition to five new youth suspense novels coming soon: *Beyond Your Control, Disappointment Meets Grace, Within My Reach, Are You Sure About This?* And *All Grown Up but Still Learning.*

Spirit of Truth Storybook Activity Page

1. *After reading the story, ask yourself the following questions:*

-   What did you like about the story?

-   What would you change about the story?

-   What could you have done to make things turn out differently?

-   Can you think of a way to help others after reading this story?

2. *Go back through the story pages and **decode** your **secret message**.*

-   Write the message on the lines below.

    -   Send it to me through email LMasonOnTop@aol.com

I will send you back a personal comment. Be sure to include your gender and age.

Dove Letter Cutout

E

25

3. ***If there are puppets in your book,*** *cut out the finger puppets and assemble as instructed. Be careful with your scissors.*

- Use your finger to help the character walk out a happy scene that you create.

- When finished playing, place your puppet characters in a zip lock bag or an envelope, and store it between your favorite pages of the book for safekeeping.

- Ask your parent or guardian if you can collect all 26 "Spirit of Truth Storybook Series" and remember to save the *Dove Cutouts* and glue them into the proper places on the chart.

Instructions for Making Finger Puppets

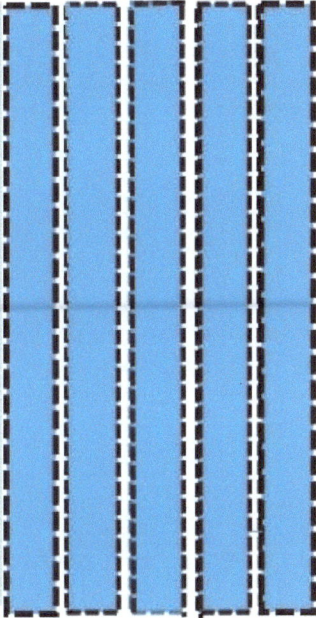

1.

Follow the dotted lines.

Cut figures out.

2. Cut strips out. Follow the dotted lines.

3. Fold over strip and tape into a ring.

4. Tape ring on the back of the figure that you cut out.

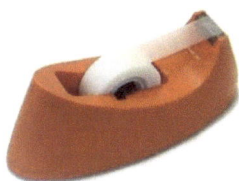

Cut Out the Finger Puppets

Cut Out the Finger Puppet

Receive a *15% discount coupon* off of the purchase of my Editor's Edition of "**The Spirit of Truth**" Storybook Series, with proof of purchase from A - Z. This special edition will contain all 26 stories within two volumes along with some added goodies. Fill out the chart below, and **please** **print** all information clearly.

A	B	C	D	E	F
G	H	I	J	K	L
M	N	O	P	Q	R
S	T	U	V	W	X
Y	Z				

Glue your "*Dove Letter*" cutouts in the corresponding boxes, on top of the proper letter. Fill 26 spaces from A- Z. Then cut this page out and mail it to:

Linda Mason

P. O box 1162
Powhatan, VA 23139

Name _____

Address _____ State _____

Zip _____ Email _____

"The more you read the more things you know. The more that you learn the more places you'll go."
-Dr. Seuss

Excited Ernesto Word search

Circle the following words

Ernesto	City Bus	Dominoes
State Fair	Money	Donte
Excited	Maria	Sister
Cotton Candy	Green Peppers	Corn Dogs
Onion Rings	Hamburgers	Roller Coaster
Hurricane	Tickets	Gloria
Restroom	Screams	Sweet Dreams

g	p	x	e	m	r	e	t	s	i	s	n	r	l	h
l	e	o	u	c	a	y	s	o	y	e	n	o	m	g
o	o	n	o	c	o	r	o	b	x	t	q	l	j	w
r	t	i	k	s	m	n	i	u	k	l	g	l	y	w
i	c	o	t	t	o	n	c	a	n	d	y	e	e	r
a	b	n	b	a	n	o	a	s	d	u	h	r	c	e
v	b	r	n	t	m	a	m	f	g	l	d	c	v	r
g	c	i	h	e	s	k	o	l	g	j	h	o	n	n
u	k	n	a	f	j	z	o	x	v	o	a	a	m	e
j	n	g	m	a	S	c	r	e	a	m	s	s	w	s
l	J	s	b	i	h	l	t	c	j	p	s	t	k	t
v	z	b	u	r	j	j	s	m	x	l	t	e	g	o
e	x	s	r	e	p	p	e	p	n	e	e	r	g	r
n	y	y	g	z	j	x	r	c	x	k	k	n	k	c
a	f	k	e	k	r	s	v	J	u	p	c	k	t	y
c	t	y	r	c	j	g	m	k	j	s	i	x	h	i
i	e	l	s	l	o	o	m	b	m	o	t	m	f	u
r	p	t	h	h	k	d	j	a	u	m	k	k	c	T
r	j	l	n	b	l	n	e	m	u	g	k	i	b	g
u	z	p	j	o	n	r	m	m	t	o	d	l	d	g
h	m	b	b	v	d	o	s	i	s	t	e	r	x	m
z	c	c	x	t	v	c	n	b	m	m	t	n	y	q
x	l	p	e	p	o	i	h	h	h	d	i	g	o	a
z	v	e	d	o	m	i	n	o	e	s	c	l	p	z
x	w	c	c	c	c	v	b	g	l	k	x	i	y	x
s	a	k	j	r	w	u	n	n	j	h	e	y	v	b

Excited Ernesto Word search

Answer Key

1	2	3	4	5	6	7	8	9	10	11	12	13	14	15
g				m	r	e	t	s	i	s		r		
i		o			a				y	e	n	o	m	
o		n			r							l		
r		i		s			i					l		
i	c	o	t	t	o	n	c	a	n	d	y	e		
a		n		a			m					r		
		r		t			m					c		e
		i	h	e			o					o		r
		n	a	f			o					a		n
		g	m	a	s	c	r	e	a	m	s	s		e
		s	b	i			t				s	t		s
			u	r			s				t	e		t
e		s	r	e	p	p	e	p	n	e	e	r	g	o
n			g			r						k		
a			e		s							c		
c			r		g					s		i		
i	e		s		o			m				t		
r	t				d		a							
r			n		n	e								
u			o		r					d				
h				d	o	s	i	s	t	e		r		
			t		c					t				
		e								i				
	e	d	o	m	i	n	o	e	s	c				
	w									x				
s										e				

I Know! I Know!

a	j	p	r	m	x	o	y	z	q	e	w	l	y
s	z	e	e	f	s	p	w	a	p	l	r	r	t
e	r	t	b	s	i	r	q	u	o	i	y	w	x
u	n	t	c	a	o	m	n	o	p	d	o	b	m
m	v	y	b	d	h	h	s	a	i	s	i	g	j
r	z	n	i	w	d	s	a	m	g	c	u	r	k
o	a	i	u	y	s	b	i	h	y	n	t	m	g
l	p	f	l	t	a	y	z	s	g	t	t	n	m
j	k	b	a	w	q	e	b	r	y	e	w	v	z

— —   — — — —   — — —   — — — — —   — — —

— —   — — — —   — —   — — — — — — —   — — — —

Find out some fun facts about the author!

Start at the circled letter. Circle every third letter and write those letters on the lines above to reveal a fun fact about the author. If you can find all seven fun facts contained within seven different storybooks and send that information to me via email at LMasonOnTop@ aol.com, you will **receive a storybook of your choice FREE.** *You only pay shipping and handling. Don't forget to include your complete mailing address, your name, and age. Have fun! (There is no answer key, so work hard).*

41

APPROPRIATE AGE LEVEL

COLOR CODING KEY

The reading level for these stories is grade five, but they can be understood and enjoyed by the ages listed below, sometimes needing to be read to by someone older.

Ages 4 and 5 = GREEN

Ages 6 and 7 = BLUE

Ages 8 and 9 = ORANGE

Ages 10 and above = RED

*A unique inspirational message has been coded throughout each story to help create 'added focus,' as well as a visual tool for interactive concentration. **Decode your secret message (written in red lettering throughout the story)** and send it to me, along with your name and age, through my email address on my website, www.BooksByLMason.com, and you will receive a personal email response from me. Some of the letters of the secret message have already been provided to assist you in your decoding. Additionally, added bonuses of finger puppet activities, brain* *games, puzzles, or other goodies, awaits each reader in the back of every storybook. A delightful "Treasure Hunt" can be found throughout the illustrations from my collection of storybooks, which **details can only be found on my website.***

Also, E-Book Editions of this collection of storybooks, having no activities in the back of the books, and a Collector's Edition of this 26 Storybook Series is forthcoming. The collector's edition will include all 26 stories in two volumes, at which time, the Master's List of every inspirational message will be revealed.

Synopsis of Each Story from A-Z

1. *Anxious Arlene:* This story is about a set of rambunctious siblings who live with their loving grandparents, and an adorable, adopted mutt experiencing a few mishaps. This story is recommended for ages five and up.

2. *Busy Benny:* Benny is a dynamic little boy who loves to tinker with wacky car models. He enters a neighborhood race one day with an impressive, wacky race car designed by himself, with the help of his parents. It's also a story about friendship. This story is recommended for ages seven and up.

3. *Catty Carla:* This story is told through the eyes of cats and deal with one cat in particular, with a "Catty" attitude. The

insults are released upon another cat that has a severe physical illness. The gossiper soon regrets the spiteful attitude and adjusts her behavior before the very sick cat transitions to "Kitty Heaven." The story does deal with the death of a pet gracefully. This story is recommended for ages five and up.

4. *Doubtful Denise:* A divorced father is raising his bi-racial daughter, who, at the moment, is full of self-doubt and lacks confidence in her ability to complete any assigned task. Through the love of her father and some very positive friends, Denise learns to believe in herself eventually. This story is recommended for ages seven and up.

5. *Excited Ernesto:* This story is about an average teen who has a fear of riding Roller Coasters. With the help of some of his friends, who also have that same fear, they work through it all at the county fair. This story is recommended for ages seven and up.

6. *Fearless Freddie:* A little boy who loves taking a risk, reminds his father of himself

when he was young. Freddie went too far one day and ended up with a severe injury, but will this stop his risky behavior or give him new ideas to participate in more dangerous stunts? This story is recommended for ages five and up.

7. *Graceful Gregory:* This story highlights the life of a young male teen who has been hassled at school because he loves creative dancing instead of football. Even his football-loving dad sometimes doesn't understand Gregory's love of ballet, jazz, and the many other facets of creative dance. One day, Gregory and his dad work things out with the help of ane teen friend who learns to appreciate the physical strength and courage it takes to become a great dancer. This story is recommended for ages seven and up, but younger if the child is already dancing.

8. *Hopeful Henry:* This story is one example of how staying "hopeful" even through rough times, always pays off. This story is recommended for ages seven and up.

9. *Itchy Irvin:* This story plays out through a pack of dog characters who encounters a

little boy with a physical problem that resembles that of his own. The dog and the little boy meets, and beautiful things begin to happen. This story is recommended for ages seven and up.

10. *Jumping Josey:* This story is about a young teen who lives a life of thrills as a cheerleader. Her hobby takes her into the arena of skydiving. This new adventure eventually leads her to a career in the Armed forces. This story is recommended for ages seven and up.

11. *Kissing Kirkland:* A very "Cutesy" story about a little boy who is infatuated with kissing every animal he comes around, including bugs. This story can is recommended for children ages five and up. This story is recommended for ages five and up.

12. *Lonely Lucilia:* This story deals with teen friendships and having to separate due to a parent's job relocation from one country to another: England to the USA. You can survive when your heart has been broken, even as a child. This story is recommended for ages eight and up.

13. *Muddy Maria:* This story tracks the life of two little girls who loved to play in the mud as children. This love of "dirty play" eventually led them to a lucrative child business dealing with plants. This story is recommended for ages five and up.

14. *Noisy Nelly:* This story is told through the eyes of a bird who learns, by the wisdom of its mother, that life is much more than things perceived as "gloomy." When you learn to see things from a different perspective, you can soar. This story is recommended for ages seven and up.

15. *Orphaned Ophelia:* Most of this story takes place in a very unique orphanage where several unrelated girls experience different lonely situations, as they all long to be adopted by a family they can call their own. Travel with Ophelia through ups and down in an exciting but lonely place where sometimes there are happy endings. This story is recommended for children ages five and up.

16. *Pudgy Pete:* This story intertwines the life of a slightly plump teen boy with self-esteem issues and an enthusiastic teen girl

who just moved in next door. She happens to use a wheelchair. Through the interactions of these two individuals, Pete's self-esteem takes on a new course, and he learns to see himself more than a plus pants size. This story is recommended for children ages seven and up.

17. *Quarrelsome Quaniqua:* This story contains **sensitive** material and is not intended to be read as a *bedtime* story. It deals with an abusive living environment (non-sexual but very much physical abuse). There are some hard times happening; however, Quaniqua does figure out, with the help of some new friends, how to turn her situation around. This story is recommended for children eight and up; however, please use parental wisdom as to if this story is suited for your particular child.

18. *Reckless Ricardo:* This story is about a young boy experiencing a reckless, behavioral unbalance due to a peanut allergy. A doctor didn't detect this. In searching the internet, one day, his grandmother (his caretaker) discovers the

real issue of dealing with Ricardo. Through a creative experiment, she was able to steer Ricardo's behavior in a more positive direction. This story can be enjoyed by children ages seven and up.

19. *Shy Stanley:* This story gives you a glimpse into the life of a tranquil little boy who has a unique talent. He channels his energy into drawing. He eventually meets a young girl who has similar skills, and they soon develop a quiet bond. This story can be enjoyed by children ages seven and up.

20. *Tearful Tanya*: This story deals with a little girl who is full of grief over the passing of her grandmother. The family has a spiritual upbringing, and Tanya's mom guides her through the grieving process as she draws strength from above, where she's convinced her grandmother now resides. This story may be a little sensitive if you are a child in a similar situation, yet it can be enjoyed by children ages five and above.

21. *Ungrateful Ursula*: This story contains 'sensitive' material and is recommended for children ages ten and above. Ursula has

become accustomed to using "Cutting" to cope with her many issues of life. Walk with her as she moves from "much pain" to "much gain." She eventually discovers a better way of coping with adversity with the help of her once absent father.

22. *Valiant Vivica*: This story is about a very gifted little girl who loves contact sports to the point of joining a coed wrestling team. Her life is interrupted by a tornado during a wrestling tournament at school. This experience changes her overall focus; however, she remains a top athlete in anything she chooses to pursue even though her aspirations have changed. This story can be enjoyed by children ages eight and above.

23. *Worrying Winston*: If you enjoy treasure hunts, you will love this story. Winston lives with his father while his mom serves in the Marine Armed Forces. They have a unique family unit, but one day Winston's worries come to pass when he gets news from the Armed Forces concerning a severe injury involving his mom. This situation changes their entire world. However, they survive.

This story can be enjoyed by children ages eight and above.

24. ***X-Con Xavier***: This person is a teen who had to be incarcerated due to destructive behavior caused by a rebellious attitude. Having had an unstable home environment, he had a "So What" attitude. While incarcerated, he encounters an individual that offers him a more positive way of life. What choice will he make? This story is recommended for children ages ten and above.

25. ***Yearning Yolanda***: This story gives you a bit of insight through the mind of a young girl who is now blind but wasn't born blind. Walk with Yolanda through an even more formidable challenge as she saves her mother's life during a house fire. Yes, even though she is blind. This story can be enjoyed by children ages eight and above.

26. ***Zealous Zeporah***: Zeporah is a very passionate young lady full of enthusiasm for life. She is also a junior coach for her track team at school. She gets injured before a vital track met but never missed a

step in leading her team to the most outstanding scores they have ever achieved. This story can be enjoyed by children ages seven and above.

About The Author

Minister Linda Mason is a unique ministry gift to the Body of Christ. Her experiences include the establishment of *Spirit of Praise Liturgical Outreach, Inc.*, a non-profit 501 © three organization, which not only helped to establish and oversee new dance ministries but also extended into the communities.

In addition to the *Spirit of Truth Storybook Series*, Minister Linda has published *Appetizers from the Word of God, Are You Hungry?* Volumes 1, 2, & 3 are excellent tools for teaching foundational truths, simplistically, from God's Word.

Linda is a native of Suffolk, Virginia, the wife of George B. Mason, Jr., the mother of three: Tamara, Tiena, and George III. She has three adorable grandchildren; Niyah, Laana, and Aaron. Linda holds an Associate Degree in Early Childhood Education and has a passion for writing. She has published 26 children's stories from A to Z, in addition to over 50 other books, including five suspense teen novels. Linda plans to have these unique stories available in both English and Spanish soon.

What others have stated about this Series

- *Author Linda Mason's book, "Kissing Kirkland," is one of a series of books that tells a delightful story with a secret hidden valuable message for children. Her stories will captivate her audience with a variety of age-appropriate activities to enhance each child's learning. As an educator for many years, I highly recommend her books!* **By Amelia Hopkins, a high school counselor.**

- *Linda Mason has done an excellent job using her creativity and insight in writing this series of books, the* **Spirit of Truth Storybook Series from A-Z**. *Each book deals with a subject or situation, such as a particular disability or set-back that a child might encounter and have difficulty dealing with. The books offer resolutions that are positive and encouraging, helping a child build strength, confidence, and maturity. The activities in the back of each book reinforce the lesson learned. The graphics are colorful and eye-catching, and each book's vocabulary is age-appropriate.*

Each book is color-coded to fit each age group, so there are appropriate books for every child's age. These are books your children will want to read or hear over and over, read by a big sister or brother. And they also have the opportunity to communicate with the author directly! I highly recommend these books for your children and grandchildren!

Nona J. Mason, a retired teacher, mother, and grandmother.

www.ingramcontent.com/pod-product-compliance
Lightning Source LLC
Chambersburg PA
CBHW042107110426
42742CB00033BA/21